The 21ˢᵗ Century Guide to Humanity

A collection of poems

By A. R. Meadows

this has been a long beautiful journey
and i am grateful that i could
create this book that is the essence of my being.
thank you to everyone who has supported me
and guided me, i could not have done it without you all.
i would like to acknowledge Jasmine for all the late nights she
spent helping me create my vision.

i am truly blessed.

enjoy.

-A. R. Meadows

Part 1: *The Cave*

life is an enigma
a confusing puzzle of chaos
i could reach the peak of happiness
feel ultimate peace
and it can all come crashing down
like an avalanche of heart break

that tiny little nettle
stays ringing in my head
she bugs me with
her *worries*
always babbling her
mouth as if...

she had something
important to say
she fills me with doubt
what a devilish girl

the onset begins
and i start to descend
into the darkness
ironically cozy...
with a specious appeal
welcoming me

i fall

all the things i love
seem distant now
as if they never existed at all
surrendering my soul to
my new home

consumed by quicksand
just trying to get up
the more i struggle
the more i become stuck

i want to get out
but no one is around
i thought i asked for help
but i couldn't make a sound

maybe i'll never be happy
maybe all the ups and downs of life
cancel out to one giant negative
the small pieces of joy seem...
insignificant to the heart ache of life

maybe happiness is a facade
that people paint on their faces
just to get through the pain.
is anyone truly happy?
or is it just something we see
advertised to us
in order to fill their wallets?

to fill their hearts
with the happiness
they long for
an endless cycle
in search for
"happiness"

...maybe what we need is *content*

patience
everything will come
with patience

...so they say

there is a plant
in the room i'm sitting in
there is me, a plant, and a cat

this simple placid space
fills my soul
more than anything else
or anyone else

i do not mind this space
i do not mind the silence

to love is to love all
to not be afraid
to love is to trust
and to trust is to heal
to be healed from
all of the heartbreak

to love is to love all
to shine with others
to understand their struggles
to love is to love God
to love thy neighbor
to love fully is to be free

you are my mirror
reflecting all the good and bad
you challenge me to be the woman
i want to be
and i love you for that

you don't love as others do
you're not cloying
and you don't call my name
off of a mountain

but,

i feel peace with you
the calm but never a storm
your actions speak for what
you cannot express
you're different from all the rest...

...although,

sometimes i want
to have someone
love me so deeply
to hear them scream
"i love you!" from the mountains
to love me full and completely
i want to be consumed by love
enchanted with their presence
one person. one soul.
and with you...

i don't know if i will ever have that

teach her to say no
at such a young age
her body is hers
she needs to know

don't throw her
into the world
without teaching her
to say no

she is a temple
a goddess of pure gold
her body is a gift
anyone would be so
lucky to hold

the words sounded sweet
coming from your lips
i craved their taste
and you were happy to supply
filling me with their
sugary goodness

though the more i consumed
the less full i got
your words tasted bitter
and my teeth began to rot

emptiness inundates my soul
and i cannot escape
it surrounds me
i want to break free
i can't...

...so i think i have fallen ill
no, i do not need any soup
i do not need any meds
but yes, I have fallen ill
i have been struck
with the darkness
of my own mind
it eats away at my heart
trying to rationalize
trying to keep myself together

on second thought
maybe i would like some soup

the presences of your
intoxicating aura
still lingers in my mind
you were a whirl wind of a ride

our stars were crossed
from the start
and it looks like
our journey has stopped

i must continue
down my own path
i'm stronger now
so i won't look back

*do not let anyone steal your peace
you are strong like mountain peaks*

she was a pool of sorrow
finding the most tragic beings
the most beautiful

she would give herself to them
trying to keep them safe
she soaked up their tears
and held their hand
all while trying to take away their pain
only to be hurt when they decided
to take themselves away

she loved the ones who couldn't be saved
ultimately leaving her with heartache
she screamed from the mountain tops
her lost brothers' names
as she is left on this earth to figure out
what it all means

their ships made the waves
that crash down onto my soul
i was treading water
just to stay afloat

until i found wood
to build my own ship
now i'm setting sail
with a ladder i kept

so when i look out
into the sea
and see someone treading
harder than me

i will have the means
to help them on board
so they do not have to
tread water any more

forever
standing on a seesaw
trying not to lean to far
one way

trying not to be polarizing
searching for perfection
but it's exhausting

always trying to think
of the right thing to say
the "right" way

i am meant to be free
my energy needs to expand
out into the universe
to reach everyone in need
my purpose is to bring joy
still, i feel trapped
like i am not where
i am supposed to be
stuck in a cage
this is not me

note to self:

in order to help others
i need to
i have to
help myself

it is the ultimate feeling
far better than happiness
far better than peace
danger with a twist of glee

love
it's make or break
and to love one's self...

is my missing puzzle piece

the lunatics come out at night
the moon lovers
the admirers all come out
to see her shine
they watch her performance
she never disappoints
her vim on display for all to watch
her beautiful gaze

Part 2: *The Renaissance*

patience is the key
if you are struggling

STOP

...breathe...

relax your shoulders
unclench your teeth

look at where you are
admire your journey so far

patience is the key
if you are struggling

we are filled with broken hearts
the jaded dreams of humanity
pour into the streets
these crushed souls swallow themselves
in other worldly things
constantly trying to escape
their reality

a hard exterior to protect their
delicate frame that has already
been bruised way too many times
always on the run
and never stopping
to heal themselves

their past traumas
ride on their shoulders
almost like a badge of honor
as if the more trauma they endure
the stronger they are and
the more success they will achieve
but strength comes in many ways
and to confront your trauma
that is intrepid

who are we to judge?
does this mollify the attack on
our own ego?

we hurt ourselves
then hurt others
take a step back

it's hard to make decisions
when you're the kindle to
your own fire

.

organic
like the earth
like the cascading leaves
from the treetop

organic
like the food we eat
or the oils we apply

but some how
no matter how
hard we try
our organic frenzy
stops at our taste buds

we are power driven
mechanical in our reactions
and in the way we climb

we are ruthless to our friends
we are vicious to our family
we lost our hearts
for the exchange of vanity

no amount of organic
will cleanse our mechanical soul

oh dear, how numb
we have become
tragedy strikes
almost like a routine
we then find humor
in these tragic things
our eyes glued to the screen
and a slight chuckle
leaves our breath
as the tragedy has turned
into a meme

we are numb
but has it made us stronger?
or has it poisoned our minds?

America –
once beautiful
...or was she ever?
masked behind the make-up
the filters, the botox
to keep up her presentation

inside she is alone
burning with self-hatred
her children wear bullet proof vests
like a fashion statement
so, they can take a seat as society
force feeds them information
while her sisters are held prisoners
in their own bodies

she has taken a million step forward
and now a million steps back
let us pray for Miss America
and hope change is on the horizon

the vultures have logged online
scrolling for their next pray
sloughing through the comments
looking to destroy someone's name

cancel culture is all they know
so, watch what you say
because if they get their talons in you
you'll be over before the next day

run.
as fast as you can
maybe someday you'll make it
don't look back because if you do
your worst fears will come after you

run.
until your thoroughly drained
this is how to be successful
this is the American way

we live in a society where
calling the cops could be a death sentence
my black brothers and sisters
are on the streets
pleading for acceptance
for something that should
have never been in question

who do you call when you
need to be saved from the cops?
who checks their balances when
they do you wrong?
how was "i can't breathe"
not enough to be said
for them to understand
they were killing a man?

we need to fight
to take back our power

                    when was it stripped from us?
                when did they burn down our towers?

they try to keep us apart
cus' they know we are stronger together

                    but we are blinded by hatred
                      and that may never feather

we must dismantle this system
it's broken to its core

                held together by money and greed
                    and i cannot take it anymore

get out of the cave
open your eyes!
you need to be awakened
do not let them
feed you these lies
we are the people
the power is in us
traditions need to be broken
so, our country
can finally be just

Part 3: *The Revolution*

she was full of
molten hot flames
it consumed her every being
it ate at her day and night
until it began to pour out
and abused the quiet space
it escaped from her grasp
as she desperately tried to catch it

but what was done, was done
she felt no regret
only a pure wave of relief
she was calm, collected
complete.

water dropped from the heavens
as peace of mind became
the new familiar feeling

all the time that i've spent
in my head has cost me

                          time i will never get back

the world in my head can ruin me
it can consume me

                          a beautiful darkened mind

i spent so much time up there
that i forgot to look around

                          blinded by my thoughts

but the clouds have been lifted
and i can finally see

                          i am finally out of the cave

the image of herself was faded
she didn't know where she belonged
she found validation through others
but the validation never lasted to long

until you are confident in who you are
until you have a clear image of your path

you may never be fulfilled

Step 1.
i must leave anything and everything that brings
negative energy

Step 2.
i will mend my relationships and learn to communicate
effectively

Step 3.
i will create a strong support system surrounding myself
with unearthing love

Step 4.
i will learn to stand on my own and not let fear keep me
down

Step 5.
i will meditate, breathe, and find peace in simplicity

Step 6.
i will put 100% into achieving all desires and will be
confident in my capabilities

Step 7.
i will change this world.

i have seen the waves crash
from coast to coast
i've lost myself and found
myself a million times
and have finally settled
on a single mold
at my young age i have
enough stories to fill
the shelves of the largest
library

the limits that society places
on you
the limits that your family places
on you
the limits that you place on
yourself

they do not exist
they are only real if you
make them real
you are the creator
of your own destiny
the power is within you

i dive into the blue ocean sky
feeling weightless
felling free
i let myself sink
until the world is lifted off my back

is this where peace lives?
is this where the overworked
underpaid brilliant minds go
when they have torched their last bulb?

i can feel the divine flow from above
connecting to me
raising my vibrational energy
it's warm breath
glides effortlessly past my face
i am weightless
i am free

the darkest places also have
the brightest light
illuminating the mind
to bring peace
to take a stand
to be largess
we are more than the limits
we place on ourselves
the potential within us is sublime

i am opinionated
i am passionate
i am extreme
who am i to deny myself
the experience of being
the most authentic person
i can be?

it's a crime to
hide yourself
to hide who you really are
in order to be pleasant
to be like able
to dim your light

because others can't see

stand.

plant your feet in the ground
be strong
what you believe is yours

that cloud of human energy
above your head

filter through the negative
only you know what is best

stand strong
you're an angelic goddess
don't let your crown fall

you are a deity in
its purest form
ground your feet
prepare for the storm

always hiding from the light
never wanting to shine too bright
seemed liked bad things followed me
cus' he couldn't let me be

trust was broken and replaced by fear
and i held that secret, didn't shed a tear
i'm older now and came out of my shell
and now, i have my story to tell

if you're scared, it'll be okay
i promise it will get better one day
it's your story so take your time
i just want to see you shine

i found strength in myself
when i left the past behind
i separated my being
from what did not serve me

i used to lean on the shoulders
of others to help lift me up
praising their strength
but never finding my own

it's easy to figure out
what is not meant for us
we know in our hearts that
it does not keep us grounded
it does not keep us sane

the hard part is letting go
and throwing ourselves
into the unknown
let go

the world has so much more to offer you

a wave of energy from one
medium to another
the way the hand curves
and glides on the paper
as if it were dancing to the
rhythm of my thoughts
and once it's complete
a masterpiece is unveiled
all because a pen meets a paper

they say that we are God's creation
we were made in his image
thus

we are godly
because God is within us
divinity shines through our souls
burning bright in this world

we were meant to create
they say heaven is for the dead
but i say it is here for the living

this is God's gift to us
and it is whatever we make it

i am older so i must be stronger
am i wiser?
another year around the sun
feels oddly like bliss
i am not the person i once was
but at the same time i never changed
instead i smoothed out the rough edges
i tuned into the best parts of me
i am happy to be 24
because i am happy to be me

when you truly love yourself
and you are genuinely happy
only happiness streams from you
it burst from your inner being
you want to share it with the world
you want to help others find it
it's beautiful. it's magnificent.
and i found it

there is a change on the horizon
the world is going to transcend
and we are coming along for the ride

everything we have worked for
all of the blood, sweat, and tears
will be for something

something more amazing than
any of us could have imagined
it's our time now
i feel it

Thank you

-A. R. Meadows

www.ingramcontent.com/pod-product-compliance
Lightning Source LLC
Chambersburg PA
CBHW032127050726
47590CB00008B/2991